Tantric Sex

Master The Art Of Tantric Sex Through Love Connecting Guided Sex Positions And Techniques, With Pictures

Max Bush

Table Of Contents

Introduction 1

Chapter One: Solo Tantra 5

Chapter Two: Setting The Scene 22

Chapter Three: Genital Practices 33

Chapter Four: Additional Positions 39

Final Words 53

© Copyright 2018 - All rights reserved.

It is not legal to reproduce, duplicate, or transmit any part of this document in either electronic means or in printed format. Recording of this publication is strictly prohibited.

Introduction

You may have heard of Tantra. Tantra is a system of ideas derived from ancient Hindu and Buddhist traditions and practices. But what about Tantric Sex? Tantric belief systems see sex and eroticism as being natural aspects of life; furthermore, sex is viewed as a path to spirituality. The Tantric view of sexuality is unabashed. Some aspects of Tantric Sex have been perceived as extreme, however they are not commonplace. This book will focus on introducing you, the reader, to the ideas behind Tantric Sex and provide a practical guide on how to incorporate Tantric Sex in your sex life.

You are probably thinking to yourself, *okay, what is the difference between sex and Tantric Sex?* Sex is often reduced to a simple, mechanical act. But we know it is, and *should* be, more than a simple, mechanical act. You want your sex life to be open; you want your sex life to help you understand yourself and your partner. Opening yourself to the Tantric practice will help you with exactly that!

But maybe you are still thinking: I do not know what Tantra is and how it plays into sexuality. Well, let's dive right in!

First, one must understand the openness of sexuality. Sexuality has oddly been a contentious issue. Sexuality is a normal part of life for most individuals, yet an embarrassment toward sexuality has existed for centuries. In recent times however, we have seen an openness toward sexuality and an understanding of sexuality's breadth. Tantric Sex is not stringent, but it does require one thing from a participant: an openness. This does not mean you need to follow everything or do something that makes you uncomfortable; rather, you should keep an open mind in your approach to sexuality.

Tantric Sex is meant for you to emancipate yourself from any boundaries. Tantric Sex believes you will reach the Divine through sexuality. Sexuality and Sexual Thought is accepted and is seen as an important facet of life in the Tantra philosophy. As mentioned above, Tantric Sex is not stringent. It is not a set of ideas that must be followed. You do not have to declare that you engage in Tantric Sex or join a group that shares your ideas. Everyone's Tantric Sex experiences and perceptions will be different. No one is more or less 'Tantric' than you are due to their perspective on Tantric Sex. Ask a hundred people about Tantric Sex and you will receive a hundred explanations as to what it is. Like the openness of the Tantra philosophy itself, the experience of Tantric Sex is also open.

There are certain sexual acts which have been popular amongst Tantric Sex practitioners. This book will provide some of these sexual acts which should help you begin your journey with Tantric Sex. These acts will also help you gain a grounding of Tantric Sex as you continue your journey and open yourself to new experiences.

As this book is intended to be a guide I would suggest you refer to it whenever possible. To ensure that Tantra remains a consistent approach to your sex life, you want to use this book as a guide which can be revisited at any time. Tantra is not a goal to achieve and as a result, there is no destination. For making the most out of this book and ensuring you follow through with the lessons provided, I would recommend keeping a notebook and pen by your side as you read. You will be referring to this notebook to practice the exercises, recording any progress, and keeping a schedule or planning ahead for the exercises. This may seem like homework, but it will ensure that you are able to make the most out of your learning about Tantric Sex and apply it to your sex life. The first chapter focuses on individual exercises, though I would recommend you have your partner read it when you are finished. If they follow the exercises and record their reflections as you do, you will both receive the great benefits of Tantric Sex together!

Tantric Sex and Tantra in general, is known to utilize factors like chakras and energy which you may or may not be familiar with. Many individuals are intimidated by Tantric Sex because they feel they need a deep understanding of a variety of topics beforehand, ranging from metaphysics, to Hindu traditions and rituals, to chakras and energy. But do not worry! This book is focused on applying Tantric traditions and practices for the modern reader. Regardless of what knowledge you may or may not have about Tantra, this book will give practices which are straightforward; an understanding of the importance of these practices and how they will benefit your sex life will be provided.

Before moving on, take a moment to reflect upon your sex life and your sexuality so far. Take out your notebook and pen and answer the following questions. Answer in as much detail as possible:

1. What was the attitude toward sexuality as you were growing up? Did you grow up in a household that had a liberal or conservative attitude toward sexuality? Or do you not know because it was never discussed?
2. What was *your* attitude toward sexuality as you were growing up?
3. What was the prevailing attitude toward sexuality in the society you lived in? Has it changed? If you live in a different society, how does it differ with your previous society?
4. If you could change other person's attitudes toward sexuality what would you do?
5. What are your current attitudes toward sexuality? Are you happy with this? Do you want to change anything about your perspective?

6. Do you experiment often with your sexuality and your sex life? Do you try new things? Do you engage in much foreplay? Do you set scenes or use toys or props?
7. What do you feel about your partner? Do you feel your partner has a healthy attitude toward sexuality? Do you wish to change anything about your partner's sexuality or their approach to sex? If you do not have a partner, describe what you would like in an ideal partner.
8. What do you think your partner feels about you and your approach to sexuality? How would you like your ideal partner to view your approach to sexuality?
9. What would you like your partner to think of who you are as a person? If you do not have a partner how would you want them to perceive you?
10. Finally, what do you already know about Tantric Sex and what are your thoughts on what you expect before moving on to the further exercises in this book?

Chapter One: Solo Tantra

In this chapter, you will learn how to prepare yourself for Tantric Sex.

You have answered quite a few questions and are now ready to explore the world of Tantric Sex! You will hopefully have dispelled any apprehension you may have toward Tantric Sex and are ready to open yourself up to experimentation and discovery. Since this book is about bringing Tantric Sex to your relationship, *you* are not the only one who must open up to embrace Tantric Sex. However, before you begin to discuss Tantric Sex with your partner, you must first open *yourself* up and make *yourself* comfortable with the practices.

This first chapter will focus on creating an atmosphere within yourself that will be conducive to Tantric Sex. Ensure that you develop a discipline with the following practices in this chapter; you will need to change your attitude toward sexuality, and therefore alter your lifestyle in order to receive the benefits of Tantric Sex. Now that you have that in mind, it is time to jump right in!

Take A Breather!

One practice essential to Tantric Sex is something you are doing as you are reading this book: breathing. Breathing is something we do all the time, and therefore we do not realize its importance; we also seldom breathe consciously. You may not realize it now, but breathing will play a huge part in improving your Tantric Sex techniques with your partner. But for now, you must master breathing for yourself.

Pause for a moment and follow these exercises to improve your breathing techniques:

1. If possible, find a quiet space where you can be isolated from others and from distractions. You may sit or stand straight. Ensure that your back is as erect as can be. Now, breathe in deeply and let your breath flow outwards by opening your mouth and breathing out heavily. Repeat this for at least five minutes.
2. Our politeness causes us to be embarrassed about yawning. But yawning is a great way of breathing out and improving our breathing techniques. Perhaps you will still want to cover your mouth or restrain yourself in public. But in your private space, practice yawning – it will have the same effect as the heavy breathing in and out.
3. Breathe and moan. This is something you probably already do during any form of sexual activity. But otherwise you would not think about breathing and moaning to your fullest extent. That would be awkward, would it not? Well, you are following Tantric Sex, and nothing is awkward! Once again, make sure you are standing or seated and have your back as erect as possible; Take in your deep breaths and hold them in for as long as you can. When you exhale moan as loudly and with as much fervor as you can. Repeat this for at least five minutes.

The above exercises should help you develop a discipline of breathing. This will serve as a solid grounding for opening yourself up for Tantric Sex and Sexual exploration of yourself and your partner. Next, we will do a silent activity: meditating!

Meditation

Meditation is very popular but is often misunderstood. This book focuses on Tantric Sex for the modern world, so Meditation will not be defined by its stereotype: that you must sit with your legs crossed, close your eyes, imagine light flowing through your body and chanting in Sanskrit. You are welcome to practice this form of Meditation of course; but, just as there are no hard and fast rules with Tantric Sex, you must understand that the same applies to Meditation.

What is the purpose of Meditation? The goal of Meditation is for one to relax one's mind. I am willing to bet that your life is hectic. The modern world presents us with many distractions and we must find a way to relax our mind and bodies. This form of relaxation is Meditation. For the purposes of this book, I want you to take a moment and reflect on what is your preferred way to meditate. Find time out of your week to practice this Meditation and be disciplined about it. If you wish to lie on your bed with your eyes closed, do so, but ensure that you can do it on all or most days of the week. If going for a run is your preferred method for Meditation, then ensure you are disciplined about going for a run and are disciplined about your run!

Laugh

Have you ever laughed during sex? Despite the absurdity of the question, I assure you it is entirely serious! Maybe you did and were embarrassed, and your partner was taken aback. Or maybe you would consider it strange if such an incident occurred during sexual activity. Well, you know the pattern by now: Tantric Sex wants you to dispel such ridiculous notions. Just as you would smile during moments of sexual gratification, why would you not laugh? Laughter is the ultimate expression of bliss; a laugh is far more expressive than a smile. Just as you have practiced your breathing and meditating techniques, you must also practice laughing!

Find your quiet space and practice these exercises:

1. Laugh out loud! Breath in deeply and let out your breath in loud, unabashed bursts of laughter. Repeat this for at least five minutes.
2. Engage in more activities that make you laugh. Whether it is reading a comic novel or watching a stand-up comedy special, fill your life with more laughter.
3. In moments of distress, laugh at the situation to relax yourself. This may not always be possible and is challenging based on the situation – but give it your best shot!
4. When you smile, laugh. As I stated before, laughing is far more expressive than smiling. So, turn that smile into a laugh whenever you can! Even a chuckle will suffice!

Focus!

The final step is to improve your focus. This is perhaps the most difficult step, but it will make you a more focused individual. Take a moment to think about your partner or a partner whom you desire; can you accurately describe their features and personality? Take a sheet of paper from your notebook and jot down your answers to the following questions in as much detail as possible about this individual:

1. Describe in the detail, the eyes of the individual. Go beyond their color: are they a light brown or are they as dark as a starless night? Are they large or small? Are they expressive or unassuming? What about around their eyes?
2. Describe their physique. Do not focus on if they are slim, average build, or heavyset. Do they have wide hips? Long legs? A puffed chest? Broad shoulders?
3. Describe their personality. Does this individual have a relaxed approach? Are they anxious? Are they reticent or boisterous?
4. What attracts you to this person? It can range from their career to how well they tell a joke. Be free for this one, remembering to be as descriptive as possible.
5. Once you have answered the above four questions in as much detail as possible, you can revisit them at a later time to add additional information/observations if you feel you can. You can also now have free reign in whatever else you wish to write about this individual. This can range from habits or characteristics they have which arouse you, to sexual fantasies you have about them, to their taste in anything from food to films. The sky is the limit; your goal should be to have an understanding on who the person is. The more detail you can provide should be an indication of how focused you are on them and who they are as an individual.

You may wonder what these particular exercises are for. Remember that Tantric Sex is considered sacred. It is intended to be focused and conscious and not a simple, mechanical act. Being able to focus on your partner and understand them beforehand will help you when engaging in Tantric Sex with them.

Before we move on, you must ensure you set a discipline of practicing the exercises in this chapter, so you have a sufficient grounding for when you move on to practices with your partner.

Turn to a blank page in your notebook; you will be creating a schedule or planner to set time aside from your week to practice the aforementioned exercises. It does not have to be fancy, you can organize your calendar as you see fit but it should follow this example:

Monday - Friday

10 AM to 10:30 AM – Breathing Exercises

12 PM to 12:30 PM – Laughing Exercises

4 PM to 4:30 PM – Meditation

9 PM to 9:30 PM – Writing (Focus Exercises)

You want to ensure you stick to your schedule as consistently as possible to guarantee you get the most benefit from these exercises.

On another blank page in your notebook, you will be keeping a Progress Log. With the Progress Log you will keep track of what you have learned and gained so far from the exercises. The goal is to observe what you are feeling from the exercises. As there is no 'right or wrong' with Tantric Sex, there are no right or wrong answers from these exercises. Here is how you can format your Progress Log:

Write the date at the top of the page. Write each of the questions below and leave a few spaces between questions to fill in your answers. Here are the questions to answer:

1. How do you feel after completing your Breathing Exercises?

2. How do you feel after completing your Laughing Exercises?
3. How do you feel after completing your Meditation?
4. Do you feel your focus on your partner or desired partner has improved since writing about their features?

Ideally you will answer these questions in as much detail as possible and each Progress Log will open a new avenue of expression. At the end of each month, take the time to read through your Progress Logs to reflect on how you have improved with your exercises and what you have learned. Ideally, each time you log your progress there will be something new.

The preceding exercises are not strictly of a sexual nature. But as I mentioned, they are essential for opening yourself up for later practices. There are more practices one can do individually at any time to prepare themselves for a sexual experience or to simply become more 'sexual' as an individual. One must always keep in mind that Tantric Sex is an unabashed attitude toward sex. I promised I would not overwhelm you with any historical perspective, but it is crucial to remember than as a tradition steeped in Hindu philosophy, sexuality is seen as a natural part of life and therefore, cultivating a healthy sexual appetite is normal and not something to be embarrassed about.

Going Solo

At any time, one should feel free to stimulate and awaken their sexual energy, whether they are planning to have sex soon or in the future – or not at all! If you decide to incorporate Tantric Sex into your life, you must be sexual. I will now introduce you to some practices which are more sexual in nature in comparison to the previous practices.

Here are a variety of practices which fall under the umbrella of self-loving or Solo Tantra, if you like:

1. Masturbation: you are welcome and encouraged to love yourself and try to provide yourself with as much sexual pleasure as you can.
2. Dressing and undressing: what clothing makes you feel sexually awakened? Is it a particular costume, lingerie, or nothing at all? You do not have to exclusively be in this state of dress or undress when you are with your partner. Feel unabashed and parade around your home and check yourself out in your mirror in the clothing (or lack of) that increases your sexual energy.
3. You are never too old to play with toys: vibrators, dildos, pocket pussies, self-flagellators, blow-up dolls etc., are all welcome for you to use.
4. Dancing: giving a lap dance to your partner is always fun as is receiving one; you can use your free time to practice a lap dance or pole dance or any form of seductive and sexual body expression.
5. Setting the scene: once you begin the Tantric Sex experience with your partner, you will learn more about environment and ambience. In the meantime, visualize your ideal setting for sex; for instance, if it is your bedroom how would you like the bedroom to look? Would you want flowers on the floor? Any particular blanket on the bed? Any music playing in the background? How will the bedroom be lit? Experiment with setting your environment to your liking. Play around

with different ideas so you are ready to set the scene for your partner.

As you embark on your journey with Tantric Sex, you must be disciplined about awakening and stimulating your sexual energy. Your approach to sexuality should be as if you were adopting a lifestyle change. If you wanted to change your physique you would approach a discipline regarding your diet and exercise. Similarly, your approach to sexuality has to follow the same regimen. Dedicate your free time to pursuing the growth of your sexual energy; you should now see it as crucial to your life and your well-being as your diet and paying your bills are!

You would have noticed by now that the phrase 'sexual energy' has been tossed around. You are probably wondering what it means. Sexual Energy can be expressed as sexual desire, virility, passion, etc. To be enjoy sex and receive the benefits of Tantric Sex your sexual energy must be awakened at all times. This is something to cultivate and the discipline of the exercises you have learned so far will help in cultivating sexual energy.

Tantric Sex is not ashamed of the body and realizes its importance. The physical is important and any notion of separating yourself from your body should be dispelled. Your sexual energy is naturally present in your genitals, but Tantric Sex looks at the body in a holistic fashion – therefore, your entire body is an instrument for sexual activity. You will think of your genitals as sexual, but do you think of your hands as inherently sexual? You may be aroused by your partners breasts, genitals, and buttocks. When you kiss their lips, you think of their lips as sexual. But what about their nose? What about their knees?

Sexual Energy

Take a moment to pause and reflect. Are there any parts of the body (yours and/or your partners) which do *not* feel sexual to you? Do you not see them as inherently sexual? Have you not utilized them for sexual activity? Have you caressed your partners body with your fingers, but not your elbow? Give it a try and incorporate your elbow in your self-loving or Solo-Tantra exercises. Utilize as much of your body as you can to explore different facets of your sexuality.

Here are some practices you and your partner can follow (separately or together) to awaken the sexual energy in your body as a whole and train your endurance towards your sex life:

1. You have learned about focusing. Now, here is a challenging exercise to see how well you can focus with your eyes. Either stand erect or lie on your back and keep your eyes focused on one object or area of the space you are in. Remaining in a prone position, move your eyes as far back as you can; follow this with looking down at your toes. Pick parts of your body to observe with your eyes without altering your body's prone position; you can look at your genitals, your arms, knees, nose etc. There are no restrictions!
2. You have used your mouth quite a lot so far. You have practiced your breathing and have even laughed out loud! I want you to continue to practice using your mouth to enhance sexual energy. How many sounds can you make with your mouth? Can you shriek? Can you make 'click' sounds? Can you roll your tongue around and produce a melodious tune? Can you whistle? Practice making

sounds with your mouth. Practice and test the limits of your tongue as well: stick it out as far as you can. Move it around on the outside. Can you touch your nose and your chin with your tongue? If you flap your tongue up and down, how long would it take until you reach a stage of exhaustion? Give it a try and find out!

3. Other things to focus on your mouth are to ensure you have a strong jaw, strong (and clean!) teeth; is your mouth usually dry? What about your lips? Ensure that you are always properly hydrated. If you need to salivate do so – you want to ensure that your mouth and its' inner components are prepared for sexual activity.

4. How often do you move your head and neck during a sexual activity? From kissing to performing oral sex, our heads and necks are crucial for sexual activity – without us even realizing it! Some exercises you can do is to move your head and neck side to side and look up and down.

5. Next, we move on to the belly. Feel free to squeeze your belly, move it around and push in and out. Much of your energy comes from your belly and you want to ensure you feel relaxed in that area.

6. Finally, ensure that your torso and lower body is in order: a) thrust your pelvis back and forth b) shake your hips c) jump up and down d) bounce up and down on the balls of your feet.

Dance!

You may have noticed that the sixth point above replicates dancing. That is exactly what we will move on to next. Dancing makes an individuals' body agile and an agile body is crucial for sexual activity. The next set of practices will revolve all around dancing!

1. We will return to your hips and pelvis! Stretch your legs wide apart and shake your hips! Begin slowly and then speed things up to as rapid as you can tolerate; do this until you are exhausted with this particular movement – but be sure not to exhaust yourself completely!
2. Arch your back and stretch your pelvis as forward as possible.
3. Lean forward and push your buttocks out as far as possible.
4. Now, put your legs together and slowly swing your hips side to side.

Additional Exercises

The next step will come in handy later on. You will learn that Tantric Sex involves a lot of activities outside of intercourse; in order for these to offer gratification you want to ensure that you and your partner last as long as possible before finishing. This next exercise will help you discipline yourself for lasting longer.

Have you ever ejaculated before you wanted to? Ever tried to 'stop it' by tightening yourself? That is what this exercise is for:

1. Squeeze and tighten your genitals. Hold it for as long as you can without causing distress and then let go. Repeat for as often as you are comfortable.
2. Massage and tighten your genitals while massaging them; do this for as long as you are comfortable. Repeat for as often as you are comfortable.

You may associate Tantra with Yoga, which in turn you may associate with chanting. Tantric Sex also entails making noises to awaken your sexual energy. You have learned several techniques on utilizing your mouth to awaken your sexual energy. Here are some more exercises which are more detailed and precise:

1. Sit or stand with your back erect.
2. Slowly blow air out of your mouth with your lips rounded. Do this for as long as you can without exhausting yourself.
3. After a few minutes to catch your breath, repeat the above step, this time try to let out a soft hum as you blow out air.
4. Raise the sound of the hum and let the vibrations flow through your body.
5. Take a pause and catch your breath.

Repeat these above exercises with two other variations: firstly, by opening your mouth as wide as possible as opposed to rounded lips and secondly, by opening your lips but letting out the air and sounds through clenched teeth.

Finally, you need to be aware of what arouses you. I am sure you feel you already have the answers for this but if someone asks you, "What is your ultimate sexual fantasy?", how detailed and precise would you be in your answer? When you engage with your partner with Tantric Sex you will be setting a scene and catering your partners needs and desires, as they will for you. Before reaching that stage, you want to ensure that you have an understanding of yourself so that you can communicate effectively with your partner. With the below questions, feel free to test out the experiences to see what you enjoy.

Here are the things to consider and experiment with, beginning with the visuals:

1. What colors do you find erotic? Is there a particular color when applied to the interior design will set the mood for you? What color clothing on you or your partner will add the mood?
2. Is there a particular design aesthetic which attracts you? Do you like lingerie with a leopard print on it? Do you like a modern aesthetic or a rustic, antiquated look?
3. Do you like a room to be filled with light or dim? Do you prefer the natural light, light by an abundance of candles, or just by turning on the switch? Does the window need a particular view or no view at all?
4. Do you like a wide-open space or a confined space? Are you more aroused by a room where you and your partner can run around in or one where you are in close contact in every corner?

Next, think about what gives you aural pleasure:

1. What tone of voice arouses you? Do you like gentle whispering or boisterous oration?
2. What kind of words arouse you? Do you enjoy subtle romanticism, straightforwardness, or dirty talk? Are there particular words you like to be called? Remember, there is no shame in Tantric Sex, so do not hesitate to communicate to your partner what you like to be called.
3. What music and sounds do you enjoy?

Of course, the primary aspect of the sexual experience is the physical:

1. Where do you like being touched the most? What parts of your body bring you arousal?
2. How do you enjoy being touched? Gently caressed? Do you like being spanked hard?
3. Do you enjoy ointments, essential oils, creams etc. on your body? Do these applying these bring you arousal?
4. Do you like coolness or heat? Would you want an ice cube pressed against your body? Would you want to engage in sexual activity by a fire?

Now, reflect and observe what smells are to your liking:

1. Do you have a particular fragrance you enjoy?
2. What smells are welcoming to you? The smell of pine or oak? The fresh air of the mountains?
3. Do you enjoy the smell of food or a drink? Do these smells arouse you?

Finally, do not underestimate the power of taste in sexual activity:

1. Do you enjoy tasting your partner? Do you like having any part of their body in your mouth?
2. Would you eat or lick any edible off your partners' body?

The above is quite a handful! You do not have to find the answers to all the questions immediately. Nor do you have to have anything set in stone. You and your partner should take the time to determine what you enjoy the most from the realm of the visual, the aural, the physical, the smells, and the taste!

Well, that is it for this chapter! If you continue to practice these exercises, it will help you prepare yourself for the experience of Tantric Sex. Now, it is time to introduce Tantric Sex to your partner. Before you do, it is strongly suggested that your partner reads this chapter as well so you both are on the same page!

It is also important to understand that these tips, techniques and ideas are all used to create a stronger physical and emotional connection between you and your partner.

Chapter Summary

- You must learn about yourself before embarking on this journey with your partner.
- Try the practices mentioned regularly to prepare yourself for Tantric Sex.
- Be aware of the senses and what your sexual preferences are.

In the next chapter, you will learn practices for you and your partner to try.

Chapter Two: Setting The Scene

In this chapter, you will learn how to prepare and awaken the sexual energy with you and your partner.

Now that you have accustomed yourself to the practices to prepare you for Tantric Sex, it is time to open up to your partner.

The best way is to share what you have learned is through your exercises with your partner. And no, this does not mean hand them your notebook and ask for feedback! You must verbally communicate how the exercises have helped you and how they have turned you on to the idea of Tantric Sex. Your openness and enthusiasm should spark an interest in your partner for Tantric Sex. Have your partner try out the exercises outlined in the previous chapter. Once your partner has become comfortable with the exercises, you should aim to do these exercises together.

Once your partner has become comfortable and has opened up to the idea of Tantric Sex – it is now time for you both to engage in Tantric Sex practices. The first step is to prepare the environment and atmosphere.

Relax!

Before moving on to more sexual practices, it is essential that you and your partner open yourselves up by warming up! As Tantric Sex is about being relaxed in order to open yourself up to experimentation. Here are some great exercises to warm yourself up and relax your mind and body:

1. I am willing to bet you have had a hectic day or have a busy and stressful life in general! This affects our sex lives tremendously. Ensure that you and your partner destress before moving on. Get rid of any negative emotions you may have; set aside any chores or 'to-do's' that are cluttering your mind. Have a calm mind. For your relaxed body, ensure that you are properly hydrated and that you have eaten properly and rested your body as it needs to be.
2. To remove any possible stresses, here are a few solutions: punch a pillow, clean any clutter, jump around, scream out your frustrations, or shake your body!
3. Ensure that you and your partner take your hygiene seriously. Have a shower or bath beforehand. Do any necessary ablutions such as brushing your teeth or using the bathroom. You should be cleansed and feeling fresh before engaging in any of these practices.
4. Dress the part! While you may be tempted to strip entirely, these first exercises are just to make you and your partner be relaxed. Wear relaxed clothing that does not feel like a burden on your body.

Warm Up

Once you and your partner have relaxed yourselves it is now time to warm each other up for the sexual practices to come! Here are some warm up practices, Tantra style:

1. You and your partner should stand across from one another. You both should be looking at each other intently. Remember the focus you observed earlier.

As you look at your partner, be conscious of the features they possess which you find attractive.
2. You and your partner should extend your arms and embrace tightly. Your arms should be around your partners' waist and their arms should also be around your waist. Ensure that your chests are pressed against each other and that you continue to look at one another intently.
3. As you hug, ensure that you and your partner have your feet firmly planted on the ground. Imagine that you are both 'one with the Earth', and that you are rooted to the ground you stand on, as a tree would be.

You can also practice the above exercise individually. Instead of embracing in unison, you can take turns embracing each other. Remember that there are no rules and you are open to experimenting and deciding what works best for you and your partner.

Next, it is time to shake things up! Hold your partner and shake their body one part at a time:

1. Wrap your hands around each of your partners' arms and shake it until they feel loose in their arms.
2. Hold your partners hands in your hands and shake them until they feel light.
3. Place your hands underneath the breasts (or nipples) of your partner and bounce them with your hands until they feel relaxed.
4. Caress and hold your partners buttocks and shake and bounce them until they feel relaxed.

Once you are both relaxed, it is time to ease the tension even more through massaging. Do this exercise to each other, taking turns with one person giving and the other receiving. While you conduct this massage, observe what makes you and your partner comfortable and relaxed. Tantric Sex is about communicating effectively with one another to understand what will bring the most sexual gratification. Here is what to do next:

1. Stand behind your partner as they bend over; massage their neck, moving down to their shoulders and finally their spine, back and inner legs.
2. When this is complete, have your partner lean their body against you and repeat the massage from the previous step.
3. Have your partner follow the above steps on you.

For the final exercise, stand with your legs stretched apart and face each other. Once again focus on your partner and look at them intently. This final exercise should be done simultaneously.

1. Breathe deeply and let your breath out in loud bursts.
2. Keep your tongue on the roof of your mouth and breathe deeply and gently let your breath out.

You can add any other exercises you and your partner wish to do. At the end of this ritual, you and your partner should feel relaxed and have peace of mind; once you are both relaxed you will be able to open up to one another and explore your sexual desires. You will now be prepared for the exciting exercises to come!

Set The Scene

Think about what would arouse you and your partner. The environment should represent that. If you both like a particular fragrance, it should be prevalent throughout the bedroom. Do you both like silence, save for the sounds you both will produce? Or should the ambience contain slow and seductive music by your favorite singers? Tantric Sex also allows for exploring options that complement sexual intercourse. What activities do you have planned to enhance the sexual experience? Here are a few that may spice things up:

A massage is always welcome in Tantric Sex. You are welcome to practice these massage techniques on yourself first before moving on to massaging your partner. Find you and your partners' comfort zone in massaging. The following exercises can be done on yourself as well as on your partner.

1. Apply pressure on the arm until pain is felt. This will determine what the threshold and the comfort zone is. When massaging, you want to ensure you do not apply the pressure which will cause pain – be aware of the pressure you are applying from when you start to when the pain is felt.
2. Practice your hugging! Do you and your partner like a tight bear-hug? A gentle embrace? Find the hugging style that makes you comfortable and adds to your sexual gratification.
3. Find a nice lotion, oil or cream which feels good on the skin for massaging.
4. Find the part of the body which arouses you/your partner when massaged: whether it is legs, breasts, buttocks, etc.

Next, think about your dressing sense. Yes, the fun part of sexual activity is to dress before you undress. Think about what makes you and your partner feel sexy. What clothing makes you feel fun, flirtatious and confident about your body. It can be lingerie or a full costume. Take the time to prepare how you look to arouse your partner. Remember, Tantric Sex is an experience not a quick act, so even outfits that can involve a bit of role playing are welcome! One person can be a police officer, and another can be a thief! The sky is the limit!

Giving And Receiving

By now, you are sure to recognize a pattern in Tantric Sex! It is a fun and playful experience. And what better way to bring fun and playfulness to your sex life than to use some toys. In Tantric Sex, toys can range from something as gentle as a whipped cream to lick off your partners body to a whip for flagellation. As Tantric Sex is open, you do not need to necessarily use a sex toy as a toy. An everyday object can also be used as a sex toy. Be creative but be responsible: not everything can and should be used as a sex toy as it can cause great harm. Experiment, but with precaution!

Once you have set things up, it is time to prepare yourself and your partner. Normally this would be referred to as foreplay but in Tantric Sex it is all part of one sexual experience. There is no difference between foreplay and sexual intercourse – all is essential to the full Tantric Sexual experience! Here is a great ritual to follow which incorporates some of the practices which you have already learned:

1. Embrace one another in the manner that you both have found comfortable and best for sexual arousal.
2. Practice your breathing exercises together. While in your embrace, inhale and exhale intensely. Then move on to inhaling and letting your breath go in loud and exuberant bursts of laughter. Then move on to breathing in deeply and moaning loudly and frequently!

3. As you are now acquainted with the areas of your partners body that arouses them, massage those areas while you are in your embrace.

Another popular form of touch within Tantric Sex is 'giving and receiving'. This has three stages. Before beginning this activity, you and your partner should strip; to make things more exciting, you can always strip each other!

Once stripped, sit across from each other, cross-legged:

1. Have your partner focus their attention on you. Your partners' arms should be rested on his/her legs with palms facing upward. Stroke their head gently and move down slowly to their neck, to their shoulders, to their arms, and finally to their hands. The rule is that they should not touch you in response – to build up the sexual energy within.
2. Give your partner a minute to relax once this activity has been completed. Now run your finger from their forehead (their third eye) to their nose. Caress their lips with your finger; Move down further and caress their chest and the nipples, and finally stroke their inner and outer thighs. Again, your partner should not touch you in return to awaken and build up their sexual energy.
3. Your partner should repeat the above steps on you now. Remember to breathe and be conscious of your breathing while doing this. As you should be unabashed now, do not worry about laughing or feeling silly while doing this activity. This carefree attitude is welcome and healthy in Tantric Sex!

One pattern you would have noticed by now is that Tantric Sex wants you to awaken your senses in order to enhance the sexual experience. Here are some exciting activities to help you and your partner activate your senses:

1. What *tastes* arouse you and your partner? Do you enjoy licking whipped cream off one another? Do you enjoy consuming fruit during sexual activity? Are there any edibles which are off-limits?
2. An essential aspect of preparing your environment, is *smell*. As I have mentioned before, maybe you can spray the room or rooms with a fragrance you and your partner enjoy. Fragrances or oils or anything emitting a welcoming smell can also be placed on you and your partners body.
3. How can you arouse your partner through *touch* by using an external implement? This goes back to using props which you and your partner enjoy. Think about other things you can use. For example, you may wish to try the giving and receiving activity from above using a feather or a silk scarf to stroke and caress your partners' body.
4. Finally, do not forget the *sound* needed for the ambience. Apart from music, what other sounds can be added to the ambience to arouse you and your partner? In addition to moaning which has been strongly advocated, are there other sounds which bring arousal: gasping, panting? Are there particular words when whispered into your partners ear will awaken their sexual desire?

Take the time to experiment and try different tastes, smells, touches, or sounds to enhance the sexual experience for you and your partner. This is what makes Tantric Sex fun!

Once you have determined what you and your partners' likes and dislikes are in regard to the senses, here is a fun activity for you both to practice which utilizes these senses:

1. Be seated across from each other as you were in the giving and receiving exercise. As with the giving and receiving exercise, your partner will be seated while you perform the activities. Afterward, your partner can perform the activities on you.
2. Feed your partner with the edibles they enjoy. Take your time in feeding them. For instance, if you want to feed them a cherry or a grape you can caress your partners' lips with the fruit. To prepare for oral practices, you can have your partner lick and suck the fruit before consuming it whole.
3. Tease your partner with smells. For example, see if you can apply a fragrance to the space between their upper lip and nose. Do this in a small dose. If the smell is something which you can hold in your palm, hold it and hold it toward your partners' nose but not directly underneath their nostrils; again, tease them with the smell.
4. For sound, play music softly but audible enough to get your partner in the mood. As your partner enjoys the music (or noise) whisper the seductive words you know they will like gently into their ear.
5. From the previous giving and receiving exercise, you should have determined what are the spots on your partners body where they enjoy being touched the most. Gently caress them in those areas.

Once this is complete, your partner can perform the activity on you.

Before moving on to the next section, speak to your partner on how you felt about these activities. What did you like or dislike about them? What other experiments would like to conduct? How would you like to alter these activities? Are there additional props you wish to use? Are there additional foods, smells, and sounds you wish to add to the environment?

These activities, if practiced, will open you and your partner up and make you understand the benefit of Tantric Sex. By practicing these activities, you will have not only enhanced your sexual life but also have understood more about your partner and conversely, your partner will know more about you. Practice these activities with your partner every now and then; as these activities can be continuously updated and you both can experiment and alter the activities to your liking, you will continue to enhance your sexual experience. These activities will prepare you for the next activities and make you feel more confident and open-minded when you approach a new sexual practice.

By now you should also be practicing the activities learned in the first chapter with your partner. Continue to observe and track your reflections of these activities to explore how you and your partner have developed. This will provide you with inspiration to continue your journey and try new avenues to enhance your sex life in the Tantric style!

Chapter Summary

- Massage is crucial for becoming comfortable for Tantric Sex.
- Set the scene and create an atmosphere which you and your partner will enjoy.
- Continue to experiment as you both explore yourselves with Tantric Sex.

In the next chapter, you will learn Tantric practices specifically for the genitals.

Chapter Three: Genital Practices

In this chapter, you will learn Tantric practices specifically for the vulva and penis.

At the core of sexual activity of course, are the use of genitals. Now that you and your partner have prepared yourselves for Tantric Sex, you will now learn about how to awaken the pleasure in yourself and your partner by focusing solely on the genitals. This chapter will cover techniques for both the penis and the vulva.

Vulva

We will begin with the vulva. If this is the genital that your partner has, you perform the following activities on them; if you are the one with the vulva, your partner can do this on you and you can also perform these activities on yourself!

Make sure the environment is welcoming for anyone who will be engaged in the activity. Once this is complete, the individual with the vagina should lie on their back, naked on a comfortable surface such as a bed. Make sure any requests, suggestions, or concerns are communicated clearly beforehand. Once all is settled, we can begin with massaging. The massage can be done with hands or with something soft like a silk scarf. Here are the steps to take:

1. The hands should be placed, palms down on the vulva, press (to the level of comfort) down on the vulva. Keep the hands pressed down on the vulva and continue to rotate around the vulva to stimulate the pleasure.

2. Find a lubricant, oil, or cream that you or your partner is comfortable with and is safe. This moisture should be applied in gentle doses on the fingers; once this has been done, the giver should gently and slowly stroke the vulva.
3. Repeat the previous two steps, however now you will move from the vulva to the labia. Press the labia (to the level of comfort) and rotate around to stimulate the pleasure. Then proceed to stroke the labia as you did the vulva.
4. Rub your palms together until you feel heat between them and you experience the tingly sensation on them. Once this has been achieved, press the labia together so they touch each other; ensure you are doing this to the level of comfort and hold the labia together to enhance pleasure.
5. Using your thumbs, massage the top of the inner and outer thighs, right underneath the waist. Do this for a couple of minutes to give the labia rest from the previous exercise.
6. As you had pressed the labia together, gently place your hands on the outer labia and gingerly spread it outward. Gently and slowly, blow air on the labia and the clitoris.
7. Gently touch the clitoris. As you touch gently, move your finger away and then touch the clitoris again.
8. Place your thumb on the clitoris and rotate clockwise and then counter-clockwise.

Take a breather and rest before moving on to the next portion. We will now move on to massaging on the inside. Ensure that the fingers of the massager are well-lubricated and are clean. As always, take precautions and ensure that levels of comfort are not broken.

1. Slowly and gently enter the vagina with one or two fingers. If more fingers are desired, you may insert them ensuring the comfort level does not get broken.
2. After entering the vagina, rotate the fingers to the right and press on the right side; then do the same with the left side.
3. Move your finger upward to reach the urethral sponge, above the vagina. Massage as you were before but be gentle and slow.
4. When on the urethral sponge, press gently and pull away. Repeat this motion.
5. Remaining on the urethral sponge, rotate your fingers.
6. As you are doing these exercises, you can also press on the vulva as you were doing before with your other hand.
7. After the receiver has awakened and is feeling aroused, stop and breathe heavily together.
8. Kissing and breathing into each other's neck increases the sexual tension even more.

These above activities can also be done with the use of a vibrator. Ensure that when these activities are being performed that you and your partner communicate; you want to ensure the most comfortable and most pleasurable experience for the both of you. When all these activities, are complete lie next to one another. This point is not for touching or further activity; lie together in your silence and breathe deeply as you did in your initial breathing exercises. You should both feel awakened sexually; these exercises, like the exercises you have learned before is for opening up and exploring your sexuality and your sexual preferences and desires.

Penis

We will now move on to sexual exercises for the penis. Just as with the vulva, the massaging and handling of the penis is to awaken the senses and arouse stimulation. The final goal is not ejaculation (but do not fret if it happens!) but to heighten the mood.

Once again, ensure the environment is welcoming for you and your partner. The following exercises for the penis can be conducted by your partner, or if applicable you may do this on yourself. Ensure that there is sufficient communication between you and your partner. Tantric Sex is about opening up and understanding one another after all.

The receiver should lie on his back in the nude. As the massages and practices on the penis take place, remember that both the giver and receiver should not feel embarrassed to breathe loudly, moan, or laugh. So, let us begin!

1. The penis should be gently stroked; this can be done with the fingers or with a soft implement such as a silk scarf.
2. Rub the penis gently using an ointment of your partners' choice from an oil or a cream.
3. Grab the pubic hair in handfuls and pull it upward in slow, measured movements.
4. Ensuring that you do not breach the level of comfort, you can apply pressure on the penis by squeezing it.
5. Holding the penis from the tip, stretch it to as much as it can go.
6. Conversely, pull the skin downward as much as it can go (be gentle).
7. Place the penis on the belly, press it down and rotate it – first clockwise and afterward, counter-clockwise.

8. With a lubricated or oiled hand, rub the penis in different directions to enhance the heat.

Ensure that while these practices occur, both you and your partner are breathing heavily as you have practiced. After these exercises, you and your partner should feel aroused and ready to explore more areas of the Tantric Sexual experience.

Take a moment to relax and reflect on what you and your partner have experienced. You should both have been taken to heights you have not been before. You will have both learned more about each other's' comfort levels and sexual desires. You are now more prepared than ever for further experimentation.

Chapter Summary

- Have an understanding of both the vulva and the penis.
- Follow the different techniques to pleasure the genitals.
- Remember that cumming is not the end goal, it is to build sexual energy.

In the next chapter, you will learn some additional sex positions for you and your partner.

Chapter Four: Additional Positions

In this chapter, you will learn a few additional positions in Tantric Sex.

You and your partner have achieved quite a lot! You have both opened yourself up and explored avenues of Tantric Sex which bring you fulfillment. Tantric Sex, as you have learned, is about experimenting. Here are some sexual positions which you may want to try to continue to explore your sexual desires.

Oral

As far as Tantric Sex is concerned, the G-Spot on a woman is within the vagina. The vagina is believed to hold Kundalini, the primary sexual energy found in women. When oral sex is performed on the woman, attempts should be made to stimulate the G-Spot by focusing on the vagina. Here are some positions and techniques for oral sex on the vagina:

- The tongue should enter the vagina and move around; attempt to touch the roof of the vagina.
- Gently, then rapidly blow air into the vagina.

- Do not forget about kissing! Recall how you learned about spreading and pressing together the labia – both techniques can be done while the labia is kissed.

To continue with kissing, the act of kissing on the lips may seem ordinary but there is a Tantric Sex approach to kissing your partner on the lips.

- With kissing, one person should inhale while the other exhales. This can be switched around afterward; ensure your lips are locked for as long as possible.

For oral sex on a man, the man should have his penis teased. Here is a great technique:

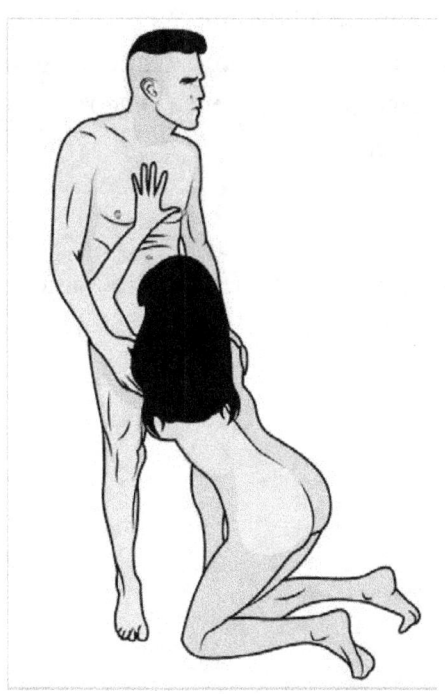

- Kiss the tip of the penis gently, then aggressively. Do it in a 'staccato' movement: kiss quickly, move away and kiss again. Repeat a few times.
- If the receiver is standing while the giver is on their knees it enhances the experience. The receiver can also hold the givers' head.

For pleasuring from oral sex at the same time you can also experiment with the 69 Positions.

Additional Positions

Here are some more positions to try out:

The Mermaid

- The giver can hold the receiver around the waist tightly; the receiver can hold on by using the givers' knees if possible; the giver will penetrate the receiver. If this is too challenging, the receiver can lie down on the bed using it as support.

Laidback Larry

- The giver can sit with one leg on the floor and the other raised up; the receiver will have their back arched and will be on all fours with their knees on the bed or floor. The buttocks on the receiver will lay on their back legs while the giver penetrates from behind. The giver can look back her partner while he spanks her and opens up his attraction and love for her.

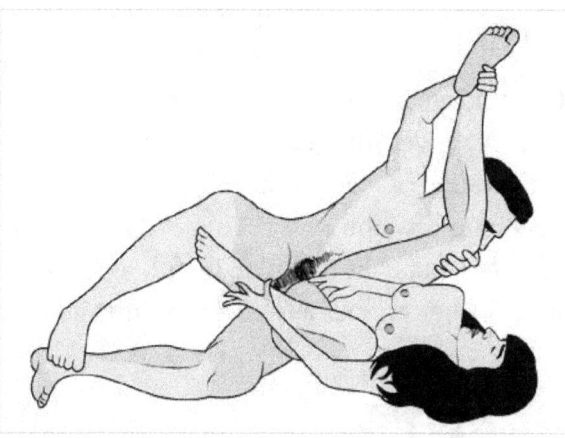

T-Bone

- For this position, the receiver has their legs in the air while the giver lies across and penetrates them; the receiver may caress and massage the givers buttocks. This Position is different and therefor hits a different angle of the vagina leading to increased sexual arousal. Talking to one another in this position is a way to increase the sexual tension also

Paddle Boat

- For this position, the receiver has their legs spread as does the giver; the receiver is seated on top. Both partners can clutch at each other's' legs while the receiver is penetrated by the giver. This Position allows the man to rest and puts the woman in full control expressing her love for her partner as she thrusts up and down.

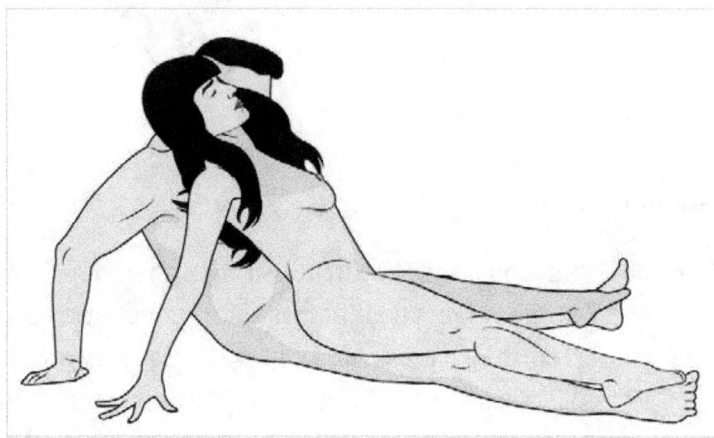

Spin

- The giver uses their hands to support themselves and has their legs stretched out. The receiver sits on the giver and can either be penetrated by the giver or can straddle the giver. The receiver may rest their back on the giver's face; in turn, the giver can kiss or lick the receivers' neck, ears and back.

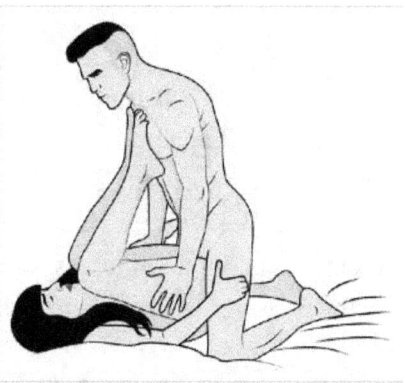

The G-Force

- With this position, the receiver lies on their back with their knees pulled towards their chest. The giver is kneeling and can penetrate the receiver. Placing a pillow under the woman's buttocks allows for an easier angle to penetrate from. Also for harder and stronger thrusts the man can either have one leg up in a lunge position or 2 legs up and feet planted in a squatting position.
- With the position that the receiver is in, the giver can also give the receiver a massage and perform oral sex as well!

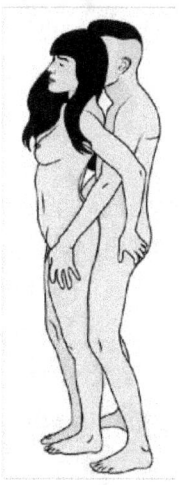

The Wall

- Remember practicing pushing your pelvis forward and your buttocks out? Those practices tie in to this position. The receiver bends forward as much as they can while pushing their buttocks out as much as possible. The giver pushes their pelvis out as much as they can. The giver can penetrate the receiver as well as massage the receiver.

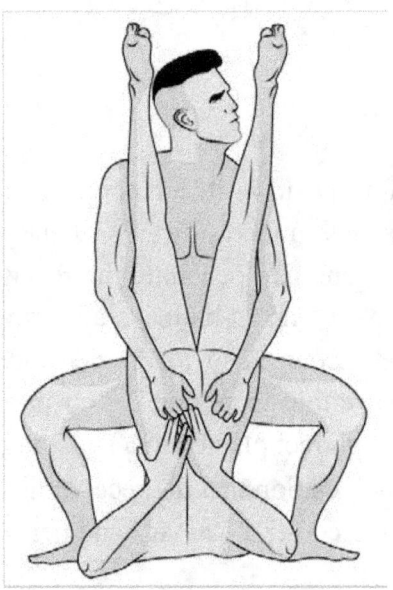

Rabbit Ears

- This exercise is tricky but it's always important to spice up the positions in the bedroom. One person will stand on their head, supported by the other person holding them firmly. The man can enter the vagina on his partner while also massaging or slapping their buttocks.
- An alternative is that the first person can also massage the second person's genitals.

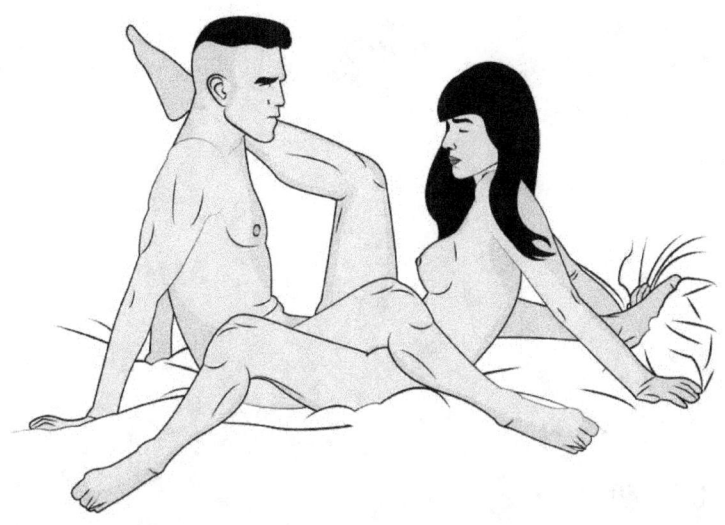

Broken Flute

- Remember one of your first experiences in this book was to sit across from your partner cross-legged? Now that you have gone through that experience, sit across from your partner and intertwine as shown in the image. Penetration is welcome; both individuals should hold each other and caress and massage each other – beginning from the neck, moving to the chest, and working your way downward.
- Slow thrusts while making eye contact enhances the Tantra being formed through one another also

Kneeling Mastery

- In this positions the man will be seated and the woman will sit on top of her partner front on in a cuddling position. This position is a very passionate and loving positions because both partners can make eye contact while they're kissing each other's neck, breathing moaning loudly into each other's ears and telling one another why you love them and what they can do to arouse you even more. If you're both into dirty talk then do that also.

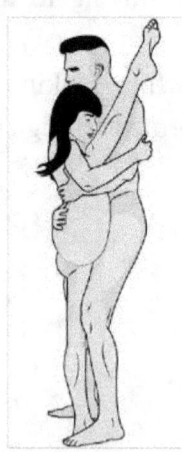

The Ballerina

- This standing sex position can be performed anywhere. The kitchen, the bedroom, the shower. The man will stand erect while the woman lifts one leg up and rests it on her partner's hip as he holds the leg up for her. Both partners can make eye contact while saying what ever they feel comfortable with.

These are the best Tantric Sex practices encouraged. Remember that Tantric Sex is open to interpretation and to experimentation. The exercises you have learned in this chapter and the preceding chapters are intended to open you up to further sexual exploration. It is all about enhancing the physical, emotional and sexual chemistry ach of you have for one another and building on the for the rest of time. You are now well into your Tantric Sex journey, and I encourage you to explore as much on this journey as you can!

Chapter Summary

- The sexual positions in this chapter can be practiced for spicing up your sex life.
- These positions are a foundation; you can continue to experiment in different ways.
- Oral sex is essential to the Tantric Sex experience for both men and women.

Final Words

Do you recall the notebook you and your partner kept at the beginning of your journeys? It is time for you both to bring the notebooks out. Here are some fun final exercises to reflect on your experience with Tantric Sex so far:

1. Swap notebooks with each other and read.
2. After reading, discuss your Progress Logs with each other. Ask each other how you have improved in the four initial exercises.

Return your notebooks to each other and answer these questions:

1. How have you felt over this journey of Tantric Sex?
2. What aspects of your sexuality did you discover? Are there new positions you found that you enjoyed? What about your environment? Did you enjoy which you did not know about before? Focus on the positive aspects, do not waste your time writing about what you did not like or care for.
3. Write about what aspects of the visual you enjoy? What did you learn about yourself in this regard? Repeat for the physical aspect, sounds, smells, and taste.

Every now and then you should reflect upon your observations. It will show you whom you were before you embarked on your Tantric Sex journey and where you are now. Tantra is about discovery and with Tantric Sex you will have learned about you and your partner's sexual desires.

Your sexual energy should now be flowing through your body. Your approach to sex and sexuality has now changed. You will no longer see it as a simple, mechanical act but as a way of life. Tantra is a philosophy that holds to a holistic and connected view of the world; similarly, Tantric Sex should make you realize that you are to use your entire body for sexuality; that having an awareness of the senses should add to your sexual experience; you and your partner will have a more unabashed approach to sexuality and will feel more gratification.

You would have also noticed after applying these teaching that your sexual and emotional connection you have for one another would have highly increased, creating a more loving and exciting relationship for you both.

I want to thank you for reading this book. Remember to refer to this book every now and then to continue on your journey with Tantric Sex. This is a wonderful journey you have embarked upon, and the best thing about it is that there is no destination – Tantric Sex is a continuous journey of discovery, experimentation, and most importantly: bliss.

If you enjoyed the information and teachings in this book please take the time to leave me a review on Amazon. I appreciate your honest feedback, and it really helps me to continue producing high quality books.

www.ingramcontent.com/pod-product-compliance
Lightning Source LLC
Chambersburg PA
CBHW072114290426
44110CB00014B/1905